Exercise!

STRENGTH

Build Muscles and Climb Higher!

Ellen Labrecque

www.raintreepublishers.co.uk

Visit our website to find out more information about Raintree books.

To order:

☎ Phone 0845 6044371

📄 Fax +44 (0) 1865 312263

💻 Email myorders@raintreepublishers.co.uk

Customers from outside the UK please telephone +44 1865 312262

Raintree is an imprint of Capstone Global Library Limited, a company incorporated in England and Wales having its registered office at 7 Pilgrim Street, London, EC4V 6LB – Registered company number: 6695582

Text © Capstone Global Library Limited 2013
First published in hardback in 2013
First published in paperback in 2014
The moral rights of the proprietor have been asserted.

Edited by Rebecca Rissman, Daniel Nunn, and Sian Smith
Designed by Steve Mead
Picture research by Ruth Blair
Production by Victoria Fitzgerald
Originated by Capstone Global Library Ltd
Printed and bound in China by Leo Paper Products Ltd

ISBN 978 1 4062 4212 6 (hardback)
16 15 14 13 12
10 9 8 7 6 5 4 3 2 1

ISBN 978 1 4062 42 13 3 (paperback)
17 16 15 14 13
10 9 8 7 6 5 4 3 2 1

British Library Cataloguing in Publication Data
Labrecque, Ellen.
Strength. -- (Exercise!)
1. Muscle strength--Juvenile literature. 2. Exercise--Juvenile literature. I. Title II. Series
612.7'4-dc22

Acknowledgements
We would like to thank the following for permission to reproduce photographs: © Capstone Publishers pp.13, 15, 17, 18, 19, 21, 23 (Karon Dubke); Corbis pp. 8 (© Gareth Brown), 9 (© Grady Reese), 10 (© Simon Jarratt), 24 (© Image Source), 25 (© Ben Welsh/Design Pics); Shutterstock pp. 5 (© wavebreakmedia ltd), 6 (© Andresr), 7 (© iofoto), 11 (© jordache), 26 (© AISPIX), 27 (© Elena Elisseeva), 28 (© Leah-Anne Thompson), 29 (© Dmitriy Shironosov).

Cover photograph of a rock climber in Red Rock Canyon reproduced with permission of Shutterstock (© Greg Epperson).

We would like to thank Victoria Gray for her invaluable help in the preparation of this book.

Every effort has been made to contact copyright holders of material reproduced in this book. Any omissions will be rectified in subsequent printings if notice is given to the publisher.

All the Internet addresses (URLs) given in this book were valid at the time of going to press. However, due to the dynamic nature of the Internet, some addresses may have changed, or sites may have changed or ceased to exist since publication. While the author and publisher regret any inconvenience this may cause readers, no responsibility for any such changes can be accepted by either the author or the publisher.

Contents

Some words are shown in bold, **like this**. You can find out what they mean by looking in the glossary.

Exercise is excellent

Exercise is excellent for so many things. It helps to keep your heart, muscles, and bones strong and working as well as they can. Exercise also makes you feel happy and look good.

Exercise even keeps your brain in top shape so you can think better. What's better than exercise? Nothing, really!

BY THE NUMBERS
Worldwide, nearly 43 million children under the age of five are overweight.

It's time to get up and get moving!

What is strength?

There are five different parts of fitness. They are **stamina**, flexibility, strength, speed, and **coordination**. Strength is one of the most important things that you gain through exercise. Your muscles get stronger through running, jumping, and playing.

Climbing also helps to make your muscles stronger.

The stronger you get, the better you become at activities. You can swing on monkey bars for longer, jump higher, and run faster. Getting stronger is definitely something to get excited about!

Warming up and cooling down

Getting stronger is great, as long as it is done safely. Always **warm up** before doing a strengthening exercise. This helps to get your muscles warm and loose. A good warm up includes gentle stretching exercises, such as touching your toes.

There are many different stretching exercises you can do.

Stretching after exercise helps to stop your muscles from getting stiff.

If you are exhausted after exercise, don't just stop or sit down. This makes your muscles tighten and makes you feel sore. Instead, do a **cool down** by stretching slowly again.

Start with your own body!

When many people think of strength training, they think of heavy weights. But, lifting weights can cause injury if you don't do it right. Lifting your own body weight is the safest way to get stronger.

You can build up your muscles by doing push-up exercises.

weights

The inchworm

Stand with your feet shoulder-width apart. Bend forward and place your hands on the ground in front of your toes. Keep your legs straight and slowly walk your hands forward, moving one hand and then the other.

Continue walking your hands forward until you are balancing on your toes. Keep your legs straight, and walk your feet forward towards your hands. When your feet are close to your hands, repeat. Try to do this five times!

MINI CHALLENGE BOX
Try to do the inchworm exercise 10 times in a row.

1

Muscles working: back, shoulders, legs, bottom, and **core**

2

Keep moving your feet forwards until they touch your hands.

Bear Crawl

Get down on your hands and feet, like a bear ready to walk. Move around the floor on all fours. Keep your arms straight, and your chest off the ground.

As a bear, you can move forwards, backwards, or sideways.

MINI CHALLENGE BOX

Move faster and run like a bear! Can you do it for a count of 60 seconds without taking a break?

It can be fun to do the bear crawl exercise outside when the weather is good.

Muscles working: arms and legs

Crab walk

Sit on the ground. Lift up your body with your arms and legs. Start walking like a crab! This exercise really works your **core**, or stomach.

Your core controls almost every exercise you do. The stronger your core, the stronger you are overall.

MINI CHALLENGE BOX

Scramble faster like a crab scampering away from danger. Can you do it for a count of 60 seconds without stopping?

Once you get used to the crab walk exercise you can start to move quicker.

Muscles working: arms, legs, and core

Duck walk

Bend your legs and get into a squatting position. Walk this way, without standing up. Wrap your hands around the back of your head so that your elbows stick out like wings.

Do you feel the burn in your legs? Try to count to 25 while you walk, before you take a break. Don't forget to quack!

Muscles working: legs, back, and stomach

The more you do the duck walk exercise the easier it becomes.

Aeroplane ride

Lie face down, flat on the floor. Lift both arms and both legs into the air, as if you are flying.

Your back should be arched and your head should be lifted. Be careful not to **strain** your neck. Hold the position for 20 seconds.

MINI CHALLENGE BOX

See if you can lift your legs and arms in the air three times, for a slow count of 20 seconds each lift.

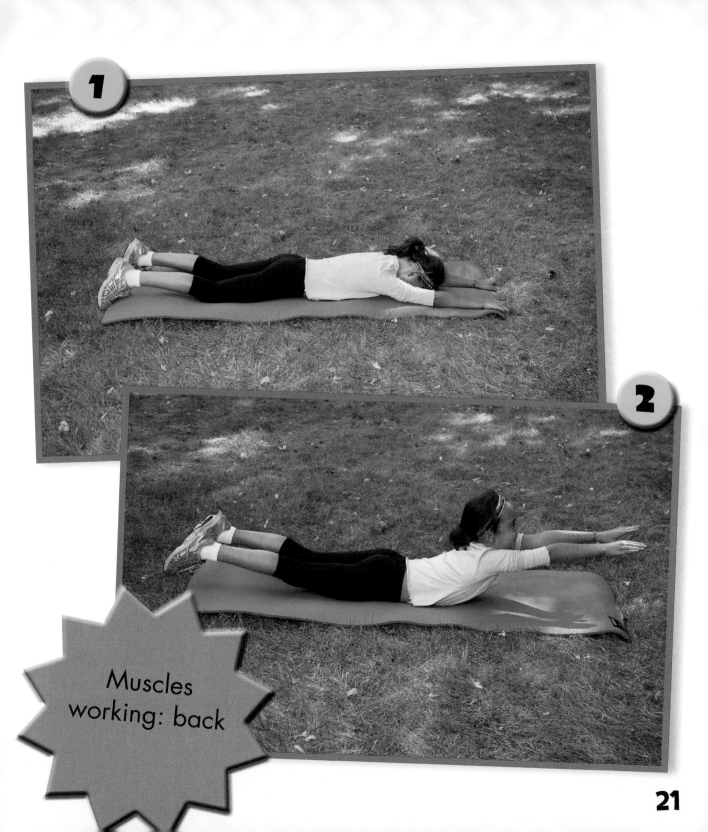

Muscles working: back

21

Circuits

Setting up different exercise stations in a park or in your garden is a good way to get a full body workout. A group of exercise stations is called a circuit. Set up about four or five stations. Each station should be for a different type of exercise.

For example, one station could be for the bear walk and another for push-ups. Try to do each station for a slow count of 30 seconds. Jog in between stations.

MINI CHALLENGE BOX

Try doing each station twice before taking a break.

When you do push-ups try to keep your body straight and bend your arms.

Muscles working: whole body

Dangers of heat

Hot weather shouldn't stop you from exercising. But it does mean you should be especially careful. It is important on hot days to drink lots of water. You don't want to become **dehydrated**, which is when you don't have enough liquid in your body to be healthy.

Make sure your body has the liquid it needs while you exercise.

If you become dehydrated, you can get **cramps**, an upset stomach, and even feel dizzy.

During the summer months, try to exercise in the early morning or early evening when it is cooler outside.

Eating well

Eating the right food is an important part of building stronger muscles. Eating lots of **protein** is one of the best things you can do for your body to help it get stronger.

 The nuts in peanut butter can give you protein.

Protein is found in meat, eggs, fish, beans, and nuts. Why is protein so good for you? It helps to keep your muscles strong and your body working.

Try to make sure you eat some foods that give you protein every day.

Big Challenge

Rock climbing is a thrilling and exciting adventure sport. There are places around the world where you can rock climb inside (on a climbing wall) or outside (on the side of a mountain). It requires bravery, courage, and strength.

Only try rock climbing in places where they have safety equipment and experts who will show you how to stay safe.

If you become strong enough and get the proper training, one day you can be a rock climber, too!

Glossary

cool down last part of a workout when the body is allowed to slow down

coordination ability to get different parts of the body to work well together

core centre part of your stomach and back. Your core helps you in almost any movement you make.

cramps pains you can get when muscles tighten suddenly

dehydrated when a person has not drunk enough water to stay healthy

protein substance in food that gives the body energy and helps it grow. Eggs, meat, nuts, and beans have protein in them.

stamina power to keep going or keep doing something

strain to harm or injure

warm up to do gentle exercise at the beginning of a workout

Find out more

Books

Athletics, Rebecca Hunter (Franklin Watts, 2009)

Exercise (Health and Fitness), Adam Schaefer (Raintree, 2010)

Healthy Eating (Health Choices), Cath Senker (Wayland, 2007)

Websites

news.bbc.co.uk/sport1/hi/academy/default.stm
Find out more about famous people in sport.

www.bam.gov
A website devoted to fitness and health for children, including exercise, safety, and eating tips.

physicaleducationresources.com/warmups_small_games_physical_education_resources.aspx
Find out lots of ideas for games and warm ups.

Index